NOTHING BUT

a series of indirect considerations
on art & consciousness

Alice B Fogel

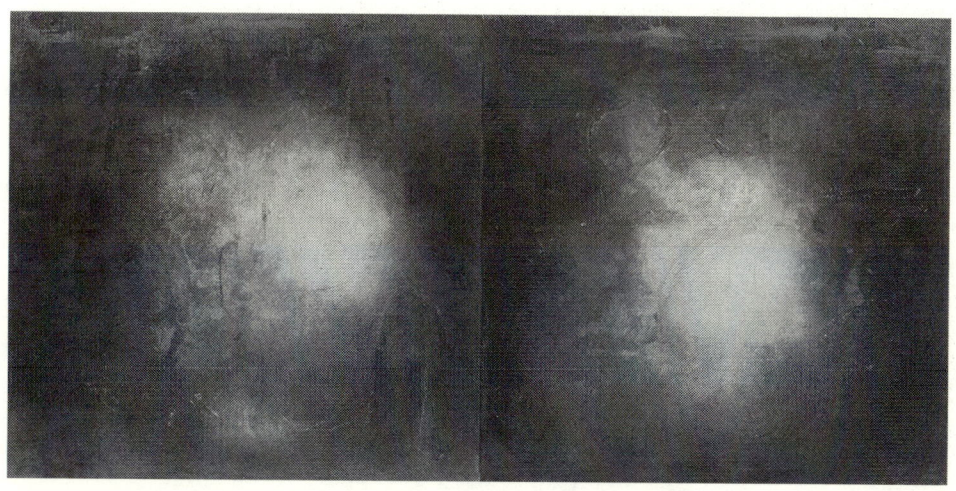

SPUYTEN DUYVIL
New York City

ACKNOWLEDGMENTS

Archaeopteryx—Glory be to the first bird
Burningwood Literary Journal—Duality
DIAGRAM—Blues
Full Bleed—Circuitry
Green Mountains Review—Notes for 59; Four Discoveries
Guesthouse—As Is; It
Hotel Amerika—Rations; One Consequence; There from Here
Indefinite Space—Spall; Inspiration; Grave Matters
Inflectionist Review—Applicable Echoes
Inkwell Journal—But If; Glacial Consciousness
Shoot the Moon, Cynthia-Reeves Art (Book)—Broken Ode; Some Place; Cornered; Between the Lines; Unnameable; Absence of Here
Shore Poetry—Ellipse
Upstairs at Duroc—Thalo Blue
Wild Roof—Om; Logos
Yale Letters—Full of Life

© 2021 Alice B Fogel
ISBN 978-1-956005-07-3
Cover art © Robin Tedesco, www.robintedesco.com, "Revelation" 2021

Library of Congress Cataloging-in-Publication Data

Names: Fogel, Alice (Alice B.), author.
Title: Nothing but : a series of indirect considerations on art &
    consciousness / Alice B Fogel.
Description: New York City : Spuyten Duyvil, [2021] |
Identifiers: LCCN 2021036094 | ISBN 9781956005073 (paperback)
Subjects: LCGFT: Poetry.
Classification: LCC PS3556.O277 N68 2021 | DDC 811/.54--dc23
LC record available at https://lccn.loc.gov/2021036094

for Jake & Sam & Mariah

CONTENTS

Notes for 59	5
Thalo Blue	6
Duality	7
Chronic	8
This Drawing of Breath	9
The 16th Objective	10
(Glory be to the first bird)	11
Applicable Echoes	13
Saving the Messages	14
On Principle	15
Amaze	16
Torn	17
Serious Elation	18
Vernal	19
(Why I crave it is because it is)	20
Touch It	21
Four Discoveries	22
Broken Ode	23
Rations	24
Untied	25
One Consequence	26
There from Here	27
(Yes it is a form)	28
Shifts	29
But Don't Stop	30
Some Place	31
You'll Adjust	32
Full of Life	33
Absence of Here	34
Uneasy Lines	35
Blues	36
(Pretend I asked the physicist)	37
On Zen Closure	38

Cornered	39
Gesture	40
Unsettled Visions	41
But If	42
Seven Times	43
Rush	44
Glacial	45
Tap Again	46
As Is	47
Om	48
(In time when)	49
It	50
Ellipse	51
Spall	52
Entitled	53
Between the Lines	54
Grave Matters	55
Inspiration	56
Floored	57
Gloaming	58
Nothing But the Truth	59
Overtone	60
Circuitry	61
Abstract Stance	62
Seachange 83	63
Logos	64
Undone	65
Unnameable	66
Art & Artist References	69
Gratitudes	73
Biography	75

Consciousness is in constant change...a series of indirect considerations....
The only breaches that can well be conceived to occur
within the limits of a single mind would...be interruptions, time-gaps
during which the consciousness went out....

—William James, *The Stream of Consciousness,* 1892

Notes for 59

when we were wordless   waving and green   taken in
   like an orphan   when we were held back from loving
       from attraction to   the line   the only division
a need for insight   when we came alive after the rain's glaze
       and saw in white clouds a black mountain and in the sea
           an inkling   that refused
       to reflect with accuracy   the predictable
elements   or when we didn't see but knew not with the fact
   but by the leap of paint   the pigment
of mineral knowing we were drawn to   and could not take
   our eyes off   even as they blinked and swept   sidelong
       and inward to find more   imaginable worlds
beyond   the given frame   it would have been easy to say
   ooh   landscape   to say *wave and sky*   or *oh*   *oh horizon*
           and feel it   as a thought
   that we had been here before   but this time   without argument
without dissembling   over a line   and with what perspective
   what indication of distance or foreground   of   what
foreshadowed   afterthought

THALO BLUE

    think about it   if it's a slippery slope   stablizing
toward the weight of color   it has more weight than thought
   when size has two dimensions   but depth of field's
      infinite as why   time's bias toward space   blue's
    toward green   a funny patch of sunlight   still
you can never expect a blue   to give you its word
    it clouds the issue it squares off   against you
and isn't talking and you can't make it   say what you mean
      when color   can't map   lacks any direction
but continuum   casts no zoom or recede   isn't a room   but cuts
   the length and breadth of the knife
        ice laden and scraped rough to the touch if you could
the edges edge   askance into darkness   the darkness slants
   through   an angle of red streaking down   parallel
     perpendicular   keep in mind
when there's something so out   of reach it could break
   if you came closer   or if only   what to consider
        what's cornered and skewed
    were ever so clearly   defined   by gold

DUALITY

it's a question of relativity
ignorant view that there are two
split down the middle a brain's
how and how not to see landscape
or hear a heartbeat an echo
a distraction from the other
and me thing and essence each
where are we even free
cut through the dry ochred earth
we need borders to cross
and again in almost
of work the transportation business
deficit and accrual an increase
effort of balancing side
is an abstraction rocking us
align to misalign
to the enormous

an exposure of the usual
sides
consciousness divided
when we look outside
detect a rhyme one
by turns stroke evoke you
requiring for identity the other
to fly over this road
this line drawn in the sand
to find ourselves again
the same place this line
a kind of attention
of possible answers in the physical
by side even eye movement
from limbic to critique
a door swung wide
all we could ever ask

CHRONIC

a long time falling through   a surface
            leaves behind the air   but this is a falling that happens
is always happening   the way we want   our lives
to go on   never falling   into place   finally
        some smudge of sunlight   clearing up   or debris
    falling through blue   broken like snow's
empty shells   between   browns hard beneath
                    something soft the sharp streaks like rays
    of scratched glass and far   away   always
coming closer coming to   a burial in   or a breathing in
    a deep and high way to never get used to falling to knowing
with our eyes closed   how to fall through that   and in
    relation to everything   especially everything blue

This Drawing of Breath

oh come on it's unresolvable   so let's stop asking   and especially   stop seeking the cheap relief
                              we'll wake up again tomorrow
                in this glitter   and stain
    or we won't   a migraine of why and is   isn't this
         how it feels   what we want   to be alive
    in light   suspended   stung
to yearn with a longing undegradable   necessary ecstacy
              of ache that has everything
     and nothing to do with us   this is it
isn't it and it's harsh and we want   yellow we want black
                          to be this infused this lit and then
from beyond that to be
       invaded by unearthly white   hot   like a flame
all the while dying   the burned out
                    stars a blindness   the sooty hard chunks
        of charcoal in the eye   in the heart   the lungs
             with unmeasurable brightness   surrounding
isn't this how it feels   this pushing
                          against the ribs from both sides
    with a force we don't even own

The 16th Objective

the last time we were wild　　　　　　and afterwards flooded with rust and mud

　we have no way　　　of being sure　　the suspended　　　moment bloats

　　　　beyond memory　　　　　　　　　　like someone else's

though what if it's not　　　about that at all　　　what if we could be

　　　splendidly got and gasping　　　for a spell　　　going to

　or coming from　　　where the glow comes from　　　unable to float

up from down　　　we could be inside　　　something difficult at the center

　　　of which is this scarily attractive　　　glimpse of the endless

stormlight　　just before or during the danger　　　uh oh

　　　so　　　　then　　　　　　　what brings us here

　　where nothing　　　　　　is obvious　　　　　and only

what makes it seem to go on and on　　　　　　the depth or the idea

      Glory be to the first bird
      in flight the last
      word winged invisible
      from the mouth

wait
what was I thinking
when I met
this art
this conjurer of
footnotes risen to head
into a dimension beyond
perception
it's like when

I watched the lines
of birds converge
to some aerial nether
neither
here nor there
a point a doused
spark of nothing a not
where sight went

out and let me in
for a while
to somewhere
other like a gasp of air
until
I felt the throb
there is no time

but there has always
been

so I crawled back in
to this tent of inner din
a useful little thinnish skin
in vastness and think
again

I deserve
these better demons
these fools and kings and ever
after

forget
that blessed bird

APPLICABLE ECHOES

                    but let's keep on trying not to talk about this
okay   just let it cross our minds
            without etching through or trickling down
even if it does   a musical score
                 that went missing   a labor of love
                         plastered over by rain
    leaked under eaves   try not to
                bring up how much the wanting
  to escape defines our staying   the context
       that haunts us   keep coming back
                to the actual applications
of our hands   what they held
  what they tried to do   before more dark fell
             the trees and other things that weren't trees
the interpretations that had nothing to do
                            with what

SAVING THE MESSAGES

because we don't know what any of it means
why do the blueprints go up in smoke
and not turn to ash   what if   inside the temple
the eternal flame still burns
because light pulses electric   then goes fluid
we stand around conferring intensely until our heads explode
we've noticed the markings
are the same as those   worms carve under bark   the maze
of what remains after they've had to swallow
their own ways   through the dark   and heaven knows
that speaks to us   we save the old broom
the bent utensil   the messages we can't read
because they're beautiful because we think
they're a part of us   then lean back
against the walls like graffiti

On Principle

```
                                             would we hazard a line
          is a parabola the way a thought          reinvented
                    doesn't recognize the boomerang when it hits
is never a line but a shading
          of an other          a dam that turns a river
into a lake from which we drink
                         more power we wish we didn't want
     here we'd almost
          risk almost ask          would     even if it fails
     to explain a thing                              or because
               under the reservoir the town still stands
with its street corners its hotels     bus stops
          and windows     all wet and quiet          not waiting
     though we're not sure where it is               we think
          color          causes          color
     to flood          to approach     would be too close
               it's cold here then it's warm warm then bruised
by seductions of paint          the line cannot refuse
```

AMAZE

so as often as we could we'd come here
                                 to let the stuff of wood and earth
scrape away the names   we have   *myself*   and
    you   come   for the counterfactuals
                                  lurk in the surface
     tension the disappearing
           which can be a little hard for us
  we would learn   the balk at the end of thought
         bitterness   in a foreign tongue
without any mood attached
                        and even that is quickening
so we'd come on purpose to aggravate
    the problem   we mean   the loneliness
       problem   the grieving   *what if*
when we look at   what we need
                  to look through   to see
    what's beyond the splintered
lens   death   the gloss   salt-streaked

Torn

                              we have to love and admit that
         there isn't always a story though surely a story
                 could stumble out of here
                             unrecognizable as a wanderer from a blizzard
        snow blind   who dies otherwise
within sight of his home   surely the out of focus
                     plots an ambivalent arc
        a physics of light and ice in which figure   the twisted
                            and turned
      testaments of glint and sheen   a green whose green
         is not rhetorical   a white that is everything but
                autobiography   in truth
is absorbing   builds suspense   tells what else   and
           if   and then and again   subtle hints
we rough in like concrete
         unwinds us like a tail   we see now   what follows
           us inside   why our eyes hurt when we look away

Serious Elation

                if you opened

        a tree   to the light

               scattered

       and swallowed its seeds

    so   at the very least   its rings unraveled

  reverberant   fungal rims

and the drench of cells   like mosaic   grew   but without

    being on your mind   and in secret the night

       or what is like night

  most of the time   never knew

           the difference

Vernal

then one element like a habitat could mean   another
         and a world
when our hot eyelids keep opening   the shallow
     algaed marsh never there before   was
depending on how the light struck   disturbing
    the littoral   distills dimensions
we can only guess at yes   we love when you don't tell us
    which   when you trouble us
with plenty enough   it is so much
    better to believe   in the yellow-swelled reds
that fuse the throat   the acid green that uncertains us
    than to waste   wishing otherwise

Why I crave it is because it is

devoid of therefore

and is not giving any given
path in some mazelike fingerprint
of reason is not the wave bored
with the moon the shore the depths

devoid of peace or proof
it is not awakening

in me a certainty
not the outcome of prayer never
the answer

that is
no

outcome no answer
not the trance the tongues
possession ecstasy the river
unable not
to find or not to find but to enter
the sea that emptying

that is at the heart
of it the necessary suspension

bridge that falls
from me as I step
away

from land not the land nor even the falling
why not
crave the pier because it reaches
only
from here

and never gets there because it takes me

now
as I am

Touch It

              what doesn't depend on time and things
        that happen in time   are so dear we want to
touch the grooves of them   with our palm
    alive and timely   to feel   what they can do to move
     us   a passport   a ticket   to where or what
to be subject to   every line   self-transplanted
    a counterpoint   we pretend to be
  a new start   a new   inclination toward want
                taking into account how peaceful it is
to be repetitive   as strata   imitating strata
     to fill the frame   continuously   newborn
  wondering   what to do   instead of focus
    on what comes all the way out to the edges
  or what it means
to believe   without lament   beyond visibility
   that ends meet   that what comes first
doesn't count any more   than what we can do
   to make   time   last

Four Discoveries

```
eros erased          everything hurt us      it was not possible
     to walk into the world without bruising
                              without covering our mouths
against heat flaring out our own skin
          we couldn't see our way          through
```

```
   accusation and flame          sure we could change
          our minds four times          five times
and still no objective
                    correlative obtained beyond the spill
     disturbing the slick lit oil     of us      we'd forgotten
```

```
     how to be                    neither naive nor ironic
how not to scar          we made of the intimate delta of veins
          a vastness or we burned
     the entire sky into a single          divided eye
               the bloodlight visible as a hand
```

```
     held up to a face          so we could not not notice
we had to collude had to wonder
                              how close we could stand
     to the singe and slash and then collapsing
between fight or flight          the intervention of blaze and ash
```

BROKEN ODE

```
          each earthen fist            remnant
    city                  comes to this and how could we
have known such a trembling
                                        encased in ash and clay
       could       hardening            go on
    to crack its own architecture       of loss
                  and decay      is so weighted to breathe
at all scrubs the invisible flesh
             in our actual throats            so dense
                                    with the material it transcribes
a thousand lives        some small sweetness
       allowed                 still              to survive
            how is it shadow       brought down
    in the creation                   to the core
       interruptive    can fall farther          into itself
               even forced up by quake
                           to be disquieted onto its physical
             plinth                when the silences
dismantling            the accidental        construction
       go on in the dark      the unpredictable
                light            inscribes        its arc
```

Rations

    every time our predilection

                                                    for thinking thinks

it would stay the same   one thing is

    how much it doesn't or we don't   then things

looking or seeming

             productive phase   into undoing

      thieving   raven in the heat   rilling off

  with our nest   in its claws everything created

    recreates   the inviolable

                        dismantles to the else a testament

to the wild

        stroke of genius a decision made

   from a distance   disinterested

 in the duel   the thing   thought

      unprepared for predator   until

    then   feathers everywhere

Untied

who or what is it   that doesn't love   a stranger
someone we could stand
         before for hours or ever and never
be able to name   even at first sight
     we get the withdrawal   from whatever came
     first or followed   whatever affection
for logic profiled   and what a line
     does is one kind   of division inviting   what binds
it flirts   with time   time is always involved
     when there's a line
     the before confessed   the promised after
a blind date so painfully perfect so tenderly
disturbing it floats   us it makes us   ridiculously happy

     to have any relationship at all   to roses   to have
bouquets of paint   we can inhale   so as to subtract the paint
     then   wow   let's pretend   it was an accident
     that we ever met
     a crazy coincidence that we recognize
each other's iterations and want   to disappear
     into their weave   we can't help
ourselves now we can't keep our hands
     off the present   we want
     to tear apart the syntheses
     unlace and spill   their silky ribbons
     rip the wrappings and fling   pieces to confettied air
get at the scents and leave   them with us when we go

One Consequence

from cell to forest
                    what we're made of that isn't   manifest
            and then is   is   a ladder without climb
an aversion to scale   so we can't parse seedling from tree
      ontogeny from phylogeny   but to worry about it
would be vanity   it's not translation but   an assemblage
we could see if our eyes didn't   use us   how deft
        how seemly   and cold   between the inky
                designs   is the negative space
of the thinking or is the thinking   the design
or we could force our hand   pull away from the things
            into their abstractions and gather
    that even if we can't tell   if we are out of the woods   yet
        all this light is coming   from we don't know where

There from Here

but does it go anywhere   else   oh   if only
you hadn't told us   but whatever   the road we took
     to get here   it's gone now   dehisced
     like a surgical wound in the otherwise
         lovely flesh   we wanted so much
to forget about this   to break
     it instead   to you   in a zeno's paradox
always halving   the distance no matter
     the never getting there   no matter
     what   where we can never go back
     it's that future we most miss
we wish we hadn't read the report
     or the name   that we could just go on   living
in the brightened silence   that islands   vernal
     into the instant   between
knowing what's coming down the road
     and the coming of it   once what was once
a lifetime   away   the initial   destiny carved seemingly
     into bark   is here   now
     a broken window become first a fountain
     of glass   next second a shrine   soon the light
after rain   and then
     what we dread   all of a sudden
     it could be happening   all
     in one mind   we're not sure which one
or one mind   could happen to it   or you
     either way

Yes it is a form
of holy blackmail this
self
induced dependency
on erasure
this addiction to intervention
its silence the opposite
of suppression fresh
running water
sourcing the feckless
revelation
revelation
after revelation
the fugitive
eventual
thought
abandoned
to lapse
the timely death
the mental mime
my *me*
unbraiding so
deliberately
its three rivers
wind
and disappear
around their bends
their best meanders
delicious
vertigoes coast
toward their dead
revelatory
ends

SHIFTS

                    and what if the world is a threshold
with no room for resistance to resolution everything would be
      is   sky   such codependent horizons
is this experience a container   am I   where would
otherwise   go the exiled   thoughts   inverted to vertical
     now there's a conversation   where
the lower atmosphere   flowers with insects mostly
to the naked eye invisible but still   knocking about and echoing
      through the gravelly hallway   of air or to diverse
    bacteria that play in our brains
a functional role   at the curbed
     diversions of the eventful
       hold back   hovering   knuckled over hints
         of some discoverable other   the polar
attractions of rare earths we covet   equally to our every
passing thought   the twain   does any of this even
   ring the bell   maybe improbable landscapes
  both too awash   or marshlike   to affirm
and too harsh a cliff to uphold   the perception of more nothing
than anything   else why   doesn't someone get the door

But Don't Stop

how it moves   out of the light suggests a window
     elsewhere in the room   we may have entered
a while thinking   to rest   then what difficult
                         relief to face no closed
clarity   that easy transparency
              that means itself   is not a means
but an end   this preferable   difference   this paradox
of vibrant and stillpoint   is a saturated gleaning
     its opacity copious   an opening   of the premonitory
possible   how the deep surface at once
          recedes and ekes   a swing
of the canvas on its imaginary   fulcrum   if there is
     where we are a barrier   between the two worlds
of foreground and distance   the art and the seeing
     it is a tabula rasa   a lapidary   turquoise and gray
          resonance on which we   might   sway

SOME PLACE

if it was the true world
            we could never live here   we could never survive
our own anxieties
     but because it's only an actual   for a while we can
still   it throws us   to go all devoid
          of our selves   and thoughts   like that
               as long as we keep winning
we cast our votes for our own oligarchy   saying
we'd be crazy not to   but sometimes   secretly
       don't we ask   *when I don't think*   am I
not   and look at the glorious   forms   we can change
  we claim   or we can love making up
everything as we go   clinging to whether patterns
           make or break us   how
literal is that thing   we undermine here   is what we fear
      afraid of us   we are hungry
          and we have imaginary friends
good ones   we haven't come yet to the point
where we lose our patience   with the trivial
    the black and white   anything but the throes
of decency   and meaning   okay   we aren't hungry now
     but we will be   we think

You'll Adjust

where are you going	stay with us	stay awake
don't go	making inroads or assumptions	use the map
provided	where are you going	to look it up

it's all ridge all whirlpool no subclause	we can't even begin
to describe how it moves	all the time it acts like it's still
where would you go	if it's time	out

of mind	a kind of temporal	immortality	to paint
	and more paint	to almost	
taste it when you try		to speak through a crack	

in the reasoning	to what hinges	what sieves
	the mirrored valley	as peered at from above
how far down it goes		how deep

the definition	its fact	the leap	don't
go to geology	to ledge	just go to the level	of paint
it shouldn't even be possible		to refuse what you see	

FULL OF LIFE

when we say *when I leave this earth*
we mean *when I leave this place I am*
and try to find anywhere   where there are no unmarked graves
we keep thinking   we're seeing   where   maybe there are none
shades of condensation   the old   horizontals
where fresh verticals of dirt   scrape away to granite and glare
a kind of feral   dusting of lichen
coats the history of the ones   buried in a hurry and left
now we can't help but doubt   and double back
make new assumptions about old assumptions
take   on purpose   everything
personally and then   we just want to cry
if we knew what makes us
conscious   if it was of atom or of   adam   if particle
or god   would that change   our minds
every time we try   we try to give up the ghost of gravity
we get so unbalanced   we're ashamed   and what
are our options
go down under humus like a seed
or be lifted   into air by heat   we're afraid
to tilt   beyond the painted limits of the frame
we have a feeling   we are the frame

ABSENCE OF HERE

```
                          it bleeds through
       like tinted walls beyond a fog           it's a rune
for art       the unreachable part      between rows knit
         in ash's bark          when we heard in god's image
    we could not    but for mirrors                 see
              what that might be       that it might be
this              now         what if we could empty to it
       take it down out of awe and abstract
a vow of doubt   that we might always    follow the gauze weave
    of its curtain     its fold and fray       because
it is so useful            this useless
       grace of material that sources      the interrogative trace
of the code for the thing itself   the precision of its teeth
                     such thingness
          that absence that bleeds through       by the truth
of its own authority                  this laying on of hands
makes palpable the infinite           field
                    of consciousness on a four-cornered
      board               the longing we bring to it
         the dream we have of it
                  the fingerprints we leave on it
 after we probe            in our sleep its flesh and blood
```

Uneasy Lines

the necessity   we don't know about that   but surely
        this strung instrument   is a fine tuned thing
there are holes to let color tones vibrate through   listening
we insist on innocence   even when a bright summer dress
        sticks to her skin as if   just shy of sky   we say a line
                and don't mean linear   then go on to wait in lines
forever   for when the music begins
            to unravel around corners   where
                it emerges or turns   we want to go to heaven
a floating   balloon's   already on its way
    we could grab ahold of its rope   that's all we've got to do
so we don't understand   what holds us back   so close
            to where we already are
                        unless it's those thrumming bars
some of us want to open
windows   some want the room air   conditioned   she is
scrambling onto our shoulders   lifting off and out
        through a skylight on a string
                    we could reach right out and strum

BLUES

because we're tired to death of blue
how it is forever
as if benignly
suggestive of depths   of   as if
it had heft   infinitude   because it is
always about some conceptual sky   as if there were virtue
in beckoning the mortal
to blame   or abandon   time
                                  we want something more
                 of blue   want a kind of blue
         that bears the limits of walls   a blue
imbued with brazen bricks flat   blackened and not beholden
    to emptiness   contextual   in its own frame   we want
             blue blurred   blue blatant   blues
                  blunt   and blared to bash
                               our brain into
its scarred substance   its thick
skin and heavy heart broken   horizoned   so much the matter
of its own making   and blindly
                  self referential   like us
not even trying to   as if it could   brush past
the fact   its burden
of blue

Pretend I asked the physicist and the mystic
    what is the nature of reality

and they said   *we cannot answer this question*
        with answers

    what if we were meant to ask
        the art galleries to arbitrate
electromagnetic actions as they orbit an exact

    consciousness   one mind

flirting with the sublime   one atmosphere
    tinged with hail and tornadoes

        and what about
the equations   will we falter when
    they fail to be as elegant
        or   worse   yield
only abstractions   heavens   no

practical applications   then will we consider
    under cover of mass and matter
        if in fact

whether in spirit we've obeyed or defied
    the given forces
  what we've had are gravity's other favors

    how what is set down can lift us
anyway
    upwards of ourselves

if we might have been capable of reaching
    entirely different conclusions

On Zen Closure

        we try not to get attached
to whether a thing   say   a rock   will float or sink
    or has already   floated or sunk   believe it
is hollow or hard   it amounts   to the same thing
    or the medium   in which we triangulate
all the way down   or up   imagining
     we can go around   and see it from all sides
  of our minds   no matter   the size   to be open to no
infatuation   to overcome   the magnetic mineral attraction
    it is no small thing   not to care
      if the seeming solidity is
the cause or the cure   of the ache   but it does nothing
  so well   how we want
      to suffice like that   we don't
know what we're doing   so in love with the physicist
  who never despairs   of significance
      or   trying to remember that
whether it is   made of meteor or cloud   dropping slow
    or fast   it is only shaped by a desire
        large enough to crush

Cornered

we
       have no   idea
    so
        we go on
           standing here on fire and not
            consumed by the flame   framed
               by our sudden
psychic exodus   this   corner   turning   turned
confounds us enough to sputter
    something about sign and signified   a device at once
fabricated and otherworldly   the colors
        of thunder and dusk and fall
    all over ourselves   out of our senses
            to exist
        it's enough
      to be in full bodied and silken flight
turned   turning
        us without referent
     to illusion   burnished
wasp nest lantern   bridal gown
    stolen by storm   one metaphor
        or another or else
          noumenon
we are at a loss
    to disbelieve our eyes for long   enough
        not to see such a thing

GESTURE

conversion's explosive's   a bouquet   a play
     on creation with the soul
         of a pile of composted october leaves
burning up after its self   combustion   a little world's
     mimicry of the universal
   gasp and release   ablur with milkweed seed
     if the gesture implies
   what's unsaid   we know otherwise
     life's all body   language   this fluent fusion
of furred wings blown upward   strokes
     of flicked liquid and marigold
   petals ripped and strewn   where did it all begin
with the erotic conception   the unfathomable inkling
  of birth   with sparked pink   the first ever
   to make contact   between canvas and brush   or where
   we came in   now space trash ignites
schematics in the exosphere   and still truth eludes us   or
     what are you suggesting   that if only faith
meant indifference to the declarative   maybe
     we'd surrender to the preemptive
   change of heart a flame   a litmus test
   we could be implicated and then dismissed

Unsettled Visions

infinity could be just another street   longer than we can see
    at every block an option
  to turn aside   under the varied slants
of roofs we keep right on   making our way
through the figures building up   overlapping silhouettes
    swatch of linen   clip of newsprint
  a box of shadow in the flattened shape
on the pavement   of its own   interruption
    the news by now   has washed out to a bleached
tissue diluting   the glue we used to stay content
      and not rupture in two
   dimensions   here we are asking at intersections
   for directions or form's corners
to take a hard line   even as   chiasmic   we'll borrow
   any substitute we come across for certainty   it's cooler
in the shade so we criss-cross   to stay in the gray
   spaces deeper   between boundaries
like walls or ground   and their illumination   later
   on an overcast day   rain could pour
    into the alleyways and we wouldn't know
all its different names   the inverted   the pooled   parallel lines
  we walk through   soaking   to change
    our downfall turned doorframe

But If

                but if it dawns on us
    we might never get it right
                        angled we'll still spin through all
thirty two petals of the compass
        rose   blown like slow tones into air
           without vanishing   we hope
    to slip between silence and its spellbound
        black into invented reds   alleged yellows
    and thank god it is always night
  somewhere   a long chain
          of dwindling notes or maybe
the gauntlet of implausibles   leads us to summer
    in a high meadow where forty thousand moths
  engorged with nectar are enough
                    to fill the grizzlies' hunger
  for a day   if it isn't science it's instant myth
because otherwise   who would believe
      one mouth could sing
    in so many voices   so much sugar
carry on the breeze as if
                we were each one in billions
  of skewed moons whose choral light comes
       from a singular point above

Seven Times

     what has already happened or
never happened but could or will   like us   is
   in thrall to the divine   madness of the possible
      use our imaginations   we'll inhale
that veil   what is the word for what
                      is not a color
  we would offer it up in place of the vagrant
        probable   never mind
your color theory   your chaos   aesthetic   we are lucky
   to be this incoherent   because   because
     what is the sense   in the imp of the perverse
inching towards the empirical and anyway what are the chances
  that could contour edgewise
       what we by turns layer and scrape
    in our craze to rend   cause from effect
lose us   in exchange for the parenthetical
   promise us we won't be gauche
        if we take colors more seriously
than we take ourselves   whether our devotion to these
  relative heavens relieves or reveals wouldn't be
      the last thing on our minds

Rush

                    in the circle

whose center is everywhere   what is the distance

       between the drenched   gold

   and its surface   the fold

         that is subject

to the eye and the one   already etched inside

    the stream   how do we bring it up

      and not get so embarrassed   with riches

    we stand   on a grand scale but still

it's the circumference   we wish we could feature

   but no   let's revel   in hopes

        fragments   left

in the arcs of the screen   will   at some point

    from the infinite   sediments wash clean

GLACIAL

what bad shape reality must be in   when we can't predict
                       what genre we're looking at
     what scale or dimension   whether
to crawl or to fly   a chance of road   heavy veins
        flooded dendrite   or delta   go figure
         because partly   we want to live
in this cognitive dissonance unseasonably taken to the vanishing
                point but not so much in the spatial
     instability where we're forced to worship except on sundays
weather's obsolete doctrine   what disturbs us is knowing
we go too far when we travel to somewhere we've never existed
       where we have to calibrate equally the record
    parameters of particle and star
country of mountains   country of deeps   the blood mystic
    reported in 3-d   we pore over and over it
   dread   its beauty   go from slough
    of despond to the predictable   highs   stumbling
in and out of focus   in and out of our right mind
    make our plans to wait out
   form   trending toward flow   a biomorphic
bellwether   clamoring   the velocity of glaciers
    winding   won't be   clearing by dawn

TAP AGAIN

if we could only know
what glass means
to birds we too might expect
to go through   we have tried
entreating every pane to let us in
to reflect what's behind us
and leave us for now
with transparency we have tapped
into these windows
with our cognitive wings
and etched our own impressions
on the glass   haven't we asked
and asked
where is that key   haven't we
turned ourselves inside out
looking
and still we can't begin to speak
to the speed of light
that had to pass us by to get here
locked as we are into mere wind

next thing we know clouds
go and shift and between the clear
intricacies we've seen up close
and the far
and blurry eternities what we think
is a wash   all innocence   one
devilish image avoids eye contact
and has no signature
while the other   suffering
sour grapes   will
chummily sign our lives away
one's the loss we hope invites us
to come over
offers a brief and sublime
flight   of thought deferred
the other breaks us in
shatters the means to return
finally
confining us to an infinite dementia

As Is

what if art makes more sense   of us than we can
    of it   if we're thirsty it's a sticky wicket to picture
or ponder the arc of the daily
        covenant with what we mean   flashing us
    its moue   we see what we want to see
                or maybe we want what we see
we see   for a while in the wilderness out yonder beyond
    the hanging gardens   we fold into the valley
    like a language for green fire   or scorched earth
      for the edges we strike between the particulates
and any way we can   we walk into the difference
  between a thought and a day   hey there's no need now
    to get petulant if it's mostly a moot path
      alas   caught in a branch   the rusted
rigmarole of memory spends itself
      free associating   dreaming its mossy dreams
of sticks and stones   if we're lucky we'll go home
    eventually   but what if the after image we catch
  is the nexus of everything
      that came before   if it's another experiment
in these woods of disorder and joy
            who cares if we don't find water
    if we do find wine

Om

        maybe the mystic by prayer goes where
the painter goes by paint and paint's blackness
    goes by shades   maybe it's discretionary
      how we render our personal tabernacles
          the dubious by its lights and not by reason
fears another's hesitation   and the greyed
    submerged is envious of flames   we lift off
           where the brush touched down
  where is your edge   what else burns
in the sanctuaries of darkened rooms   and what is
      that pregnant silence   maybe another thought
    not yet mortal nor yet ambiguous   soon
        into the material   will be born

In time when

at the brink of one island a sudden

surf's swelled
current
closed over me
my feet
sinking
into a gallery
of sand
and my eyes kept
to the dark
keening
of what I couldn't understand

I stopped

for one second

asking *what*
and *why*

and looked

and the suffering
was
only one of a thousand things

still there

It

it is almost at the harbor when we strike a precarious
        balance on the brink of a surface we call cliff
and then again we play it safe and settle   inland
    and wait for it   initially   in its wake   a bit
        of an idea scribbled into waves cracks
us open a slit   it's like we're paper   it's that easy
  to tear into us   in time   after our little pas de deux
    with denial even its vapor
        can obliterate us   it's a catalyst for remembering
at last every repressed memory of what maybe
          hasn't happened yet   it bids us
           to travel as if over hills and seas to a different
    self so we aren't at home and that's how we know
what we felt before   it's in the itinerant glow
        in the transformative *oh*   the way the smoke
proposes at once to several shades of gray and brick
        it's common sense   we insist   to believe
  in a shared reality   that reiterative   imitable
systematic illusion of certainty that's only the tip
           but it's not a foregone conclusion
     in anyone's prefrontal cortex that curiosity actually
is precarious a risk akin to the contrary   and comparing ships
      we arrive in the end   with this   it isn't
  really like anything   it's neither in the least a harbor
        nor even a brink   but is everything it is
estranged from anything but the exiled
           and for a while we welcome it

ELLIPSE

what does it even mean   to *be good*
          to be big   to do the right thing   to not leave
    the table before being excused to not leave your trash on the beach
to not speak   what you mean unless you mean
      this one little kindness that transpires   despite yourself
          how good is it not to see   how to see who we are
meant to be   it is no picnic to be left out
          in the elements all night without a blanket
      under all that starlessness   so maybe
                    it was a little wrong that we left the bottle
on purpose   buried up to its neck   in sand but it's not our fault
      that the whole ocean completely   couldn't get ahold of itself
it keeps on running its finger   along the land   and the land
      winces and shrinks
            a little more each day   see
      wouldn't it be good   to be in two shapes
    in two places at once or the one   between them
      the way a line is maybe   a horizon or a message
even if it never reaches   where we are because of course it can't
      help but be at cross purposes with us
  we get that   because sure we want enigma   we want
to be interrupted   but what if also
                    we can't stand it and we just wonder
    what on earth   do people talk about anyway
        do they just make things up in order to push back
like some einsteinian   dark energy against the inward collapse
      we'd probably be good   and   relatively   stay put too
    if we could only be a little universe   always expanding like that

Spall

at the scenic fourth wall   where the rain leaks down
   not everyone gets wet   not everyone   appreciates how
                     if not for the streaks unraveling
we couldn't see through them
                    to these yarns and their praxis enacting
      the twists and stitches of play
      by omission or ovation or by   the certitude of every stroke
of luck or clock we scrutinize on a slide
                the microbes and moth holes   the spall
     shed from a sentimental sweater   precious
and geological as mica from a stone
                       each turn and tumble is a singular
     plural scraped from a greater stage
                  more of itself than itself
   is it catalyst or catastrophe   this going on with the show
       in spite of its operatic never-after episodic ending
             its encoreless rehearsal   how are we anyway
     supposed to know through our tears   what to feel
or what to mean   when we haven't read an actual script
                       and we don't remember our lines

Entitled

>   half the way down
> through the needles   the ephemera   and fringe of bells
>   we'd forgotten   you the god we didn't understand
> and written off   the one we thought we did   we are stuck
>   deserving more   and we want so much
>   to pen you   a letter about it
>   and all the times so little happened
>   that we could say   probably
> you would have told us   you told us   so
>   you would have told us   we haven't got a notion
>   or a lick of sense   at the end of a thread
>   *not it* every one of us said
>   pinned as we were   to the whole grim mess
> of possibility   that we were
>   but you didn't contact us at least
>   as far as we could tell   to tell us   how
> many angels it takes   to get a single one of us up
>   and out of this thimble's crater

Between the Lines

through the broken wall of thought fall
in all directions shadows
away from us we call them
as we see them not as they are
since from minute to angle
of light we don't know
what they are it's a puzzle
how the poltergeists slip
in and out of human form
whatever is not gnomon
is what we by means of seeing
see erased despite being as we are
of many sound minds
we are almost a wreck
when a draped skeleton speaks
a kind of pig latin for *I* but who
doesn't believe a mirage meaning
the medium of this earth vegetable mineral
so much waste of time
delivers to us a new message
its translation immaterial

GRAVE MATTERS

    because the thought is so like a body
a possible way to remember   if we could climb
                      would be to climb
  on the rough rocks of the sky   when our eyes get
encrypted with cravings we can't depend on
        the creviced scripts wet with blood and dew
  hold on   we're still thinking   the mind's
dagger is a dagger   always there
  the way the moon is there even when we can't see it or see it
through our double vision   there is a light but not that
which is not heavy here is its shadow a lit lamentation over loss
  there is that   gravity always falls away from it   gravity is
what   freehand   makes a perfect circle
      flatten to ellipse what makes branches and birds
  wondrous   what makes the stab
    of sun for the vine the opposite force of attraction will we
ever   wake up   in the undreaming
    without want
      body cut loose from mind   half the time we fall for
half the time   because it's less solace than it is
    effort toward   happiness is why we climb

INSPIRATION

plainly without presentiment   herds of buffalo cleared
our first roads   stamped into underlayment
  grass and stone   and made for us those
shining sashes of lack   of what there otherwise was
   as all that isn't love is a lack of love   without
     compromise we followed   as if stepping
    with our own sweet feet laid a descant
    over ground a gloss on matters of time
      and space and vow   at the crossroads
     of now and then   we long to balance
   on the variants of wind sounding their crux
in every canyon   between us and still
cast a credulous eye   over the brink
    absence   is a kind of annotation a route
   we can't agree upon
     but we can take   along
      some measure of compassion
        by knife   on foot in
       wishful   intention to get
      somewhere we carve
      markings of our world
       into the markings
        of the world

FLOORED

where we apply resistance against inertia

                                          light levels lines elsewise

    than entropy   it seems so unscientific

      a budding chaos blooming in every construction

nor does believing everything will align

                                make you holy if all that zeal is really

    lack of faith   a reaction to fear   you can clean it up

    so it looks like certainty

                          but you still don't know what it spells

its acronym   its alphabets or interstices

    how many stories it will hold   to take control we uncurl

our tape measures and elevations to scale

        the work's phrenology

the shape of a thought the shape of a nail

                      driven home without a blossom

GLOAMING

what with so much weighing on it a mind
    can fall asleep become a limb   stranded and still
                              awaiting the sensations
  of mind and meanwhile
               waves of ink and parallax
crash and spill   a little cellular   triangulated
    between pinpoints   of skull but more a torch
that burns a portal in the retina   what is a hazing
       of the mind a drop from a needle into myrrh
  an exile without tracks   green bruises to almost
  black   radiates or   what it is
a mind gone *huh*   reappears   elsewhere
    like electrons   like spiritus   it comes
and leaves a residue   or a rumor   of thrill

NOTHING BUT THE TRUTH

```
            our fingerprints also will leave records
they say
                    even when moss grows over manholes
   and nonverbal ferns furl
          through the asphalt cracks      you say
it is what it is and without a doubt            that's true
      but what if      it isn't      with one
   what watermark what axiom     outlasts what's last
                and         and         and
says the nomad        in what we know
       as perpetuity          otherwise      we say
              think of the lost
   potential      but don't think
that makes it good or bad              right or wrong
       an agnostic     couldn't recognize in a line-up
   his own kind     of belief      so who can judge
the full story from some half-truth
            the freed self goes around
   saying    empty      empty      empty     and then
              caught      falters    fills
   cordons off    that whole street           it's a crime
```

OVERTONE

wherein lie our predicaments
        that we stole or that we don't know
    what was stolen   whether it was fate or fate
is the consequence   whether it is hot   alive   this wire taut
    from one nebula to its twin   thought   and not-thought
        which is where the beauty is   is it
   because optics told us   that we saw it with our own eyes
      because the metaphysics strand
          an exoskeleton over the broken body
of light   describe a form that doesn't begin
   to contain even rain   that the illusionist's
      hints   his directions drawn for distance
leave us out of our depth   we swear it was attached but to what
 if anything   we believed the sturm und drang
    entreaties from the gods   of other galaxies
   because in our ears   they rang atonal or precise
whether transmission   or interference spoke to us
  intentionally or by chance   from that unbearable babylon
      why   we could not help ourselves

CIRCUITRY

by night we played and rode   its gridlocked flow pattern
           this is where   wherever it wasn't
      already bisected   we split
the astral ground   in our bare feet
   our unbuttoned shirts and dirty   party dresses
             threads of guipure lace torn on an intricate system
        of corset bones   we circled
the aerial rose gardens   bowed   and curtsied and followed
              closely the buried turns of worms
in this fashion   by night   we leapt the hidden neighborhoods'
   irrigation ditches   took every courtyard
           and path   electric   we generated
apertures and cracks   a full blown map
       of grass and streets   paris canals
            and city trees   a million orchestral moons
   ringing and strumming with light   this is why
before dawn   night by night   we were radiant and damp
     with dew   how   wrung   unstrung   we grew

ABSTRACT STANCE

happenstance of human endeavor   spill   or weather infinite
     and limit   the art of what we see   the art of what
      happens next   for example these
raised spackles are analogies   for skin and oh we want to touch
   where the gold ends and purple begins   because suddenly
     we believe with fervor   our hands could feel
what our eyes feel   because suddenly we notice
     the darker blue   where it browns up over yellow beside
where the angles remind us of something   we intend
          to return to   has entered
and is caught in our ribs   it pleases us that catch that
    rough surface the brilliant afterthoughts   all we notice
pleases us not necessarily for what we notice but because we do

Seachange 83

                  lichen won't replace the rocks
     that host it   let's just say there is no lost
cause   world acts upon world   and we see through
      the cracks because we make them
            make and remake the way to see
    is this the way   it is   or this   when we lay down
we displace   when we wave we radiate
             each successive and simultaneous draft
the wind's own reasons to fling
      yellow pollen to skim the lake   and the lake
   still its wet delve   air's filmy vision
  moiréd over shade   light's slim spill's unlike
either memory or amnesia   or is like both
          say the brainstorm acts upon hesitance
   till interruption's interrupted
  world transformed and world unchanged
 and we   the betrayed   belied by betrayal

Logos

what could you mean
by avalanche by moss or mildew   by window
our thoughts weep through
so many frames to a vanishing   we'll fall in love
and falling   reconcile
everything ravishing   with a replica of gestures
the form the body makes as it divides
the sky   a line   a sine wave   a flaw
repeated in the architecture   of recovery
why   you mean   it's all in your mind
well   so   everything
and nothing is   priceless crisis
of yearning   pure dirt
glazed with weightless trespass   all the returning
innocence   and endless   depths of glass

UNDONE

      still today   blinded at the crossroads
                            the desert monks
might recognize for what it is
                      another impenetrable prayer
    inside the hot tents of their robes
          the melting candles of their bodies promise
there is nothing that isn't abstraction   once
    we are maddened enough   wick'd
        flames in risen heat smolder invisible
as their skin   released
    under their own cognizance   ardent
and losing patience   they might with only a flicker
    of irony decide
        that all answers are the answers
  to all questions   or that it's legit
if the redemptive blip   is subtle   a pitched pebble
    to the skull   but we want it to be
      a holy conflagration   its bright streaks
arcing in the dark   a breakage
      in the act of happening
  every time we don't look again

Unnameable

           why waste precious time worrying if
arc or cup whether streak or stream   do you understand
    what we mean   by green   why keep wanting
answers to why this why that why rose why scratch
                              and who is what
  we pretend we don't pretend when we name
when we imply or provide   a personal pronoun for what is
     a gnostic art
   we substitute name for knowing
         as if to gender what is without need of it
as if to represent what is   without us within
     because we don't have time
          not to frame the limitations of our senses
   we come to   these windows so it's as if at last
  we're giving up our eyes the better to figure
the unformed   forfeiting our fingertips to texture
    the tints of an invisible god
here we can name pigment melted light name light
   umber name umber shape shape dimension
        where we can move out of time and place
  till finally we're able to see   nothing   and to be
   uncertain
     where we are or when   or why
what is as if solid and what is like water or shadow what is
   foreground or foregone
         conclusion or the question

ART & ARTIST REFERENCES

Notes for 59: ANDREW MOORE: "Field Notes, No. 59"

Thalo Blue: JERRY TETERS: "Thalo Blue"

Duality: JERRY TETERS: "Untitled on Two Boards"

Chronic: CORIN HEWITT: "Recomposed Monochrome"

This Drawing of Breath: SUSAN OSGOOD: "Egypt Drawing 11"

The 16th Objective: BRUCE MURPHY: "Adult Object #16"

Applicable Echoes: RAGELLAH ROURKE: "Echoes at Twilight"

Saving the Messages: SUSAN OSGOOD: "Saved Messages 18"

On Principle: LIZ HAWKES DENIORD: "Principle I"

Amaze: JUDITH GREENWALD: "Labyrinth"

Torn: KATHY BURGE: "Torsion"

Serious Elation: PAULA OVERBAY—Constellation Series #9 & 10

Vernal: BRUCE MURPHY: "Tarpon Springs"

Touch It: SUSAN SCHWALB: "Toccata #42"

Four Discoveries: ROBIN TEDESCO: "Discovery I-IV"

Broken Ode: JUDITH GREENWALD: "Etude 2"

Rations: JUDITH LINDBLOOM: "Alive in the Society of the Rational"

Untied: KATHY BURGE: Untitled

One Consequence: SHIRA TOREN: "Sequence #1"

There from Here: NANCY RUTTER: "Garden Farm Road"

Shifts: SHAWN DULANEY: "Shift VIII"

But Don't Stop: NANCY HAYNES: "stopping place"

Some Place: ELLEN ROLLI: "Summer Place"

You'll Adjust: ROBIN TEDESCO: "Your Eyes Adjust to the Dark"

Full of Life: MEGAN CHAPMAN: "Pocket full of live wires"

Absence of Here: MEGAN CHAPMAN: "The absence of fear"

Uneasy Lines: HIROSHI TACHIBANA: "pink line, squeezy line and lines"

Blues: ELLEN ROLLI: "Black and Blues"

On Zen Closure: JENNA BAUER: "The Frozen Enclosure"

Cornered: JUSTIN R. LYTLE: "V (Turning Corners)"

Gesture: JENNA BAUER: "Untitled Gesture"

Unsettled Visions: JENNA BAUER: "Sunsets and Television"

But If: DEBORAH KRUGER: "Butterfly Effect"

Seven Times: MARTHA REA BAKER: "Chronos VII"

Rush: ANNA VON MERTENS: "Gold Rush"

Glacial: FRAN BEALLOR: "Gongotri Glacier, India"

Tap Again: JINNI THOMAS: "Tapestry III & IV"

As Is: JAN SESSLER: "Oasis I"

Om: JUSTIN R. LYTLE: "Looming"

It: ANTIEL PLOSZ: Untitled

Ellipse: JENNY NELSON: "Ellipse"

Spall: KATHY BURGE: "Spall"

Entitled: HIROSHI TACHIBANA: "Untitled"

Between the Lines: DIANA AL-HADID: "Divided Line"

Grave Matters: JINNI THOMAS: "Gray Matters I"

Inspiration: STONEY LAMAR: "Muse"

Floored: ANN PIBAL: "LALALALK"

Gloaming: ELISE ADIBI: "Gold and Graphite Aromatherapy Painting"

Nothing But the Truth: EMILY WEBBER: "Alethiology"

Overtone: FRANK AMMERLAAN: "Oldtown"

Circuitry: WANDA WALDERA: "Night Circuit 2"

Abstract Stance: RIVKA KATVAN, abstract protofolio painting #12 of 23

Seachange 83: SUSIE REISS, "2011.83"

Logos: PETER WEGNER: "Mineral Logic III"

Undone: LORNA FILIPPINI-MULLIKEN: "London Street 8"

Unnameable: LINDA E. JONES: Untitled Wax Study No. 8

I am grateful to Spuyten Duyvil for giving this manuscript a home, and to the editors who first chose to publish some of these poems. A huge thank you to artists of all kinds, and particularly the artists who inspired this project by your works. Some have no idea you did so, despite my best efforts to let you know; some I consider friends; and others generously corresponded with this immoderately enthused stranger. Of those whose artwork is included here, I especially bow to the two most dear to me, Fran Beallor and Deborah Kruger, for your art, your example, and your life-long friendship. For endless conversation, pretty much since you each were born, about the nature of consciousness and other unanswerables, love and appreciation to my brother Brian Fogel and my son Jake Edson. I also thank with all my heart you who so enriched my life while I wrote this book, and beyond, sharing the thrill, the relief, and the transcendence we find in the arts: Lesle Lewis, Patrice Pinette, and Ron Letourneau.

ALICE B FOGEL was the New Hampshire poet laureate from 2014-2019. She is the author of five previous volumes of poetry, including *A Doubtful House* and *Interval: Poems Based on Bach's "Goldberg Variations,"* which won the Nicholas Schaffner Award for Music in Literature and the New Hampshire Literary Award. Her book *Strange Terrain* is a guide to appreciating poetry without necessarily "getting" it. A recipient of fellowships from the National Endowment for the Arts and the Carl Sandburg National Historic Site, among other awards, her poems have appeared in many journals and anthologies, including *Best American Poetry*. In addition to her freelance reading and writing workshops, she provides academic support for students with learning differences at Landmark College, and hikes mountains whenever possible.

Made in the USA
Middletown, DE
13 February 2022